Here Today & Gone Tomorrow

I dedicate this book with love
to Dominic, husband and companion
of twenty-four years.

I hear the greenfinch singing beyond the rain,
but sweeter is your voice to me, so speak again.

Here Today and Gone Tomorrow

by BESHLIE

Broomsleigh Press

52 Lincoln's Inn Fields, London

© Beshlie Heron, 1978
ISBN 0 904646 18 1
Printed in Gt. Britain
for The Broomsleigh Press
(Fudge & Co. Ltd), London.

Contents

Foreword

Seated in our trailer-caravan on a piece of development-company owned land on the outskirts of a Northamptonshire industrial town, with the threat of eviction in a day or two's time hanging over us, the Wind on the Heath seems somewhat polluted by the strange variety of the neighbouring activities of the surrounding factories in operation, and those still under construction. However, this is the kind of stopping-place which we and many other travellers have come to accept as being perfectly normal nowadays; and for us, for the Scottish travellers with whom we arrived, and for many others scattered throughout the country, whose livelihood depends on the proximity of towns, this is preferable to the constricted regimentation of the council-run Gypsy Caravan Sites. The latter are generally placed in the least salubrious position it would be possible to find; and on these the denizens live a sort of run-down half-Romany life, depressed by the lack of space and freedom, the trailers neatly lined up on slabs of concrete just like a permanent caravan site for gaujes. That is not the real travellers' life-style, and those who submit to it generally do so after so much persecution by council-officials and police that there is no alternative.

Beshlie, myself and countless other travellers, however, do not ever pull-on such places, preferring the temporary accommodation of roadside verge, lay-bys, car-parks, building-grounds and green lanes. We travel all through the seasons, from one end of the country to the other; sometimes in company with other travelling-people and sometimes on our own. It is the *feeling* of freedom that counts; that we are beset by the problems of earning a living, providing our trailer-caravans and motor-vehicles, is all part of the pattern of the way of life . . . the returns are worth the endeavour.

My wife Beshlie and I have known the whole cycle of the travelling-life, from horses and waggons, to chrome-encrusted, modern travellers' trailers. One often pines for and regrets the passing of the old-fashioned ways and the more leisurely pace of the horse-drawn days, but it would be somewhat pointless to adhere to them purely out of a sense of ded-ication, no matter how aesthetically rewarding such a life was. It would be

7

the life of the dilettante escapist as opposed to that of the professional travelling-man of to-day.

Travelling-people, like any other branch of society, are of many groups and classes; yet all are sharply distinct in their own minds from the gaujo (non-traveller). And all are *proud* of this separateness. It is perhaps unfortunate that the 'Real Romany' of romantic fiction is rarely to be seen and recognised . . . though he is often used by officialdom and disillusioned journalists as a weapon to be used against his less obviously Romany brethren. One wonders if, in years to come, when many immigrants have inter-crossed with natives of this country, one will read similar comments?

British travellers are not all dark-skinned, black-haired or soft-spoken. But this does not mean that they are merely half-breeds or diddikais. Most travellers on the roads of these islands can trace their families back for generation upon generation, with a pride and accuracy which few gentlemen in the House of Lords could rival!

Perhaps some of the poems of this volume will bring to the reader glimpses of a way of life hitherto unknown, both in the past and in the present. They are the work of a gifted and unusual person whose simplicity and honesty of expression in word and line are so well matched by the way of life she leads.

To travelling people, always appreciative of artistic talent, the works of Beshlie are a continual source of pleasure and amazement . . . from her very decorative wire-work birdcages, her exotic dress-making and designing, melodian playing and scrolling and lining-out of waggons and carpentry, to the personal inspiration of her wild-life and herbage-filled drawings.

Without a studio, or a permanent resting-place her life is *lived*. It is good that it is so.

Dominic Reeve

8

Introduction

I would like to tell you a little about the poems. These are divided into five parts. The first pertaining to the travelling life, inevitably overlaps the second, *vers libre* of the travelling people; especially so in the poem 'Lena'. So please regard the divisions rather like a stable-door with only the lower half closed.

The persevering reader will find repetitions in the themes of the more familiar birds, mammals and plants. It is not that one does not see the wax-wing, night-flowering catchfly or otter, but they are not now as much part of this way of life as the robin, dog-rose or rabbit. The bustle of a Romany encampment, the sudden appearance of noisy strangers, frightens away the shyer creatures. The more common hedgerow birds, accustomed to lay-by and verge traffic, are, like the good-time girl, less sensitive.

It is deep within quiet fields and woods, where the travelling people are no longer permitted to live, away from the over-zealous council grass-verge cutter, or alongside the new motorways, where all humans are forbidden to linger, that one now sees the more rare flora and fauna.

Part three features some of the various itinerants one meets upon the roads. I refer to the genuine wayfarers, who are actually living a nomadic life, not to the summer crop of hitch-hiking students, whose patched and ragged apparel and bare-footed wandering might well cause one to suppose they were in the last stages of dire poverty. I have written about those who have never been granted financial support and have really known hard times, whose trouser hems are fringed by wear. The week-end tramps or week-end gypsies, the welfare children, or as the roadsters call them, the well-fed, strive to invent the privations so unwillingly experienced by the wartime generation. I leave them to their play-acting roles, we do not include them in the brotherhood of the roads . . . until they turn professional.

The fourth section is verse dedicated to the wild flowers. Revisiting places sometimes after an interval of six or seven years, I have noticed the rapidly diminishing numbers of the wayside plants; a lane in Oxfordshire, which fifteen years ago had over thirty species, this year had but five cranesbills in three miles! People ask how they can help with conservation, I suggest they collect seeds from flowers they know will be cut down, and sow them in a corner of the garden, seeds from these new plants can then be sent in letters to friends, or taken out and sown on more suitable ground.

From a large number of love poems I have selected a few that I am as happy and proud to share, as I am his life, with the man who not only wrote the most honest accounts of the horse-drawn and the motorised travelling life, but was actually living it at the time (as opposed to doing so in order to gather material for a book, or having settled-down, writing reminiscences). Like Borrow, he reported what happened practically as it was happening.

Dominic has seen Romany babies christened and then been present at their weddings. Well aware of the fickleness of human nature, it is the length of time a person lives continually like this, which counts with the travelling people, who have seen many try and fall by the wayside within a few months. Others have written romantic whimsy about the life they do not lead; we are only concerned with the truth. The keystone of the traveller's bridge is the ability to shoulder full responsibility and work for himself, anywhere, everywhere, while being constantly moved-on.

Beshlie

Part One

THE TRAVELLING LIFE

MORNING IN THE FOREST

I can touch the white spears of the frosted gorse
From the tiny window above the bed in the wooden waggon.
I can see the Winter sun casting yellow shadows,
Starred in thick clusters on the gorse.
I can hear the rondo of the skylark's morning song,
As he soars above this grassy place, impervious to all.
I can smell the sweet scent of the burning gorse fire
As the flames claim last year's bleached stumps.
Hooves drum, wheels rumble, harness jingles as travellers
Emerge, bright clad as the cock from his roost,
To drive their trollies into town for the calling,
Along the icy gorse-fringed road.

Time: January
Place: Hampshire
Romany terms: Calling, or 'going out', is knocking on house doors to sell wares or
collect rags or scrap.
Notes: A pleasant scene has now gone forever, since those who wished to preserve the
New Forest have carefully catered for visitors and livestock, but not the travelling
people, whose traditional stopping-places are now 'picnic areas'. No one actually *living*
on the roads can live or holiday in the suburbanised reserves. There is a ban on commercial vehicles!

LENA

Lena sits upon her trailer steps
Sipping a well-deserved cup of tea.
Her dark eyes upon the colourful washing
Blowing and crackling upon the line.
Row upon row of bright towels,
Frilled pillowslips, flowered sheets,
Billowing clothes of every kind.

Lena climbs the metal steps, washes
And wax-polishes the outside of her trailer.
Washes and polishes the stainless steel
Panels, bows, valances, trimmings, wheel-arches.
Rubbing until every inch shines as new.
Inside, the formica and cut-glass sparkles,
Water-cans, pail and bowls,
Handles, lamps, all fittings gleam.

Lena goes outside her palace-on-wheels
Down the carpeted steps and platform;
She is collecting the spotless washing.
Her children play on rugs in clean dresses,
The baby sits in his expensive carriage.
No housewife could have worked more hard.
A bus full of rowdy, untidy school-children
Passes, dirty derisive faces grimace,
'Gypos', and 'dirty gypos' they yell.

Time: February
Place: Devon
Notes: The travelling wife devotes herself to keeping her children and the trailer clean. Constantly in the proximity of roads or moving upon them, dirt and grime seep in. She has no running-water, no sink (they are thought to be unhygienic), no bathroom or separate kitchen.

COLD AND WET

The icy grip of gull-white frost, swirl
Of muffled mist has departed with the night.
Bold brown and white cows graze, tail to wind,
Rain-washed bright as new calves.
Pink-brown mounds of the first ploughed fields
Interlock with winter-grass hills.
Cattle trodden, cattle eaten hills, hay-brown
Wet, dead-thistled and lawn-short.
Black shining hedges, stiff, new-clipped as
Show-jumps, tall and springy as woven lattice.

From the lee of the tangled briar comes the
Mournful cry of a lone bullfinch.
Hungry long-tail tits hunt the sycamore
Branches, calling, keeping contact.
The moisture laden sky is empty of birds, only
Dripping woods, spinneys and hedgerows
Hold their tiny feathered bodies.
A local robin site, scoldings muted, a
Damp fire-ball. Oh relentless rain-wind!

Time: March
Place: Somerset

MOVING-ON EARLY IN THE MORNING

The morning dew lay like tinsel over the land,
White mist swirled about the twisting hidden river,
Marking its erratic course. Brittle-legged
Herons fished silently in their shroud.
The train, like a carpeted toy, chugged
Round the track, circling the foot-hills, hooting
Its last owl call. Wheeling rooks left
Their welkin roosts, collecting each other
In a black snow-ball; vanishing stridently
In the direction of their feeding-grounds.

A single pigeon, flying softly high, made
Swift way towards the faltering sun.

Suddenly, out of the mist flew
Seven white swans. Their glistening
Bodies catching the first golden rays as they rose.
Seven brothers, seven Princes? whispering away.
Bare now the river without them.
Speedily we ourselves depart, passing still-dreaming
Sheep, quiet dew-drenched steers. A cock pheasant
Precedes us with dignified hastening, his long
Wet tail bouncing above the hawkbit heads.
His was the road before, and his will the road be after.

Time: April
Place: Suffolk
Romany terms: Leaving a stopping-place and setting off on the roads, is referred to as
'moving-on'. Travellers do not say 'we moved', but 'we muved', no matter what their
regional accent.

Beshlie

PEACE

Rocked in the cradle of the sun
Small hessian fields lie at peace,
Minding their own ups and downs
Enjoying another uneventful day.

Elm shadows of the morning begin
To creep to the bramble-tangle hedge.
The leaning white-walled farmhouse
Bides a gull's swoop away.

Bright metallic beetles travel
The metal road, waiting and silent.
Pink chiffon clover turns to brown;
The magpies forage in pairs again.

Tall yellow mustard will vanish
Before the tough grass of Autumn.
Bright colours on a tattered butterfly
Glisten like recaptured memories.

Time: July
Place: Huntingdonshire
Note: Whilst raising their brood Magpies fly singly, but resume flying in pairs once their parental duties are over. This is a welcome sight for the superstitious who take serious note of the rhyme 'one for sorrow, two for joy'.

TRAVELLERS' LORRIES

Once the men 'minded the time'
When they had 'the bestest gry,
Pull any waggon, wheels locked'.
Eyes water, imperfections forgotten.

Now the mechanical vehicles stand
Silent, untethered. Fed with bought fuel
Not grazing free the roadside weeds.
Watering the ground with pools of oil.

Draw-bars rest where tails swished.
Wingmirrors gleam where ears twitched.
New and old, good or bad, cleaned
Discussed and invariably hard-driven.

Change hands and colour frequently,
Gain a history, are remembered,
Living out in all weathers,
Running errands and the television.

Relied on for moving the trailers.
Gaining whole families a living.
Worked and saved for, used like
Their predecessors, wildly.
'Showknees', 'mouthorgan', 'brazen-faced',
'Three-penny bit', 'frog-fronted', 'Tip-cab Ford',
Affectionate nicknames for metal horses
With polished oak bodies and double plates.

Time: September, *Place:* Scotland

DUSK

The hazel canes rattle in the withy
Bed above the bank.
Diamond leaves fall, closing
The long-empty shoshoi holes,
Forced by the indecisive wind into
One last wild dance.

We sit in the cropped-verge, bracken
Bounded lane,
Crouched up-wind, over the fiercely
Bellowed fire.
Flame fingers move rapidly up and down
Playing the wood.

A whirl-wind in the ash-fringe, scatters us
With grey snow.
The wind-king rakes the clouds, above
The vanished sun,
By whose invisible courtesy we see the
Carmine patterns change.

Time: October
Place: Bedfordshire
Romany terms: Shoshoi . . . Rabbit.
Notes: Withy-bed is a place where willows grow. The word withy means tough but flexible,
which well describes the willow wands used for making baskets. Small baskets made of
hazel canes are sometimes referred to as withies.

CHRISTMAS TIME IN THE OPEN

The first snow has come and gone,
Leaving ribbon and penny floods
Across the saturated land.
Crinkled brown paper oak leaves
Cling stubbornly to knotted branches.

The mist-rain never tires, all is damp,
Fur, canvas, shoes, harness, clothing,
Horses, dogs, birds.
Berry-bearing shrubs are overloaded,
Hawthorn, hazel, holly, sloe, each branch
A clustered, fruity taper.

Bantams down-tailed, cocks and hens
Alike, sad and miserable in
The everlasting chilly bath.
The fire is high and bright below the
Mat black kettle, its gold heart
carrying our life along.

The dreary scene is saved by colour,
Scarlet wheeled trap, yellow waggon,
And blue water-carriers.
Above the wind and noisy flapping,
My greenfinch and linet, joining a
Wild cousin, puff themselves in song.

Time: December. *Place*: Yorkshire

20

SALISBURY PLAIN

Violent winds rock our canvas cradle,
Bleak and bare the well-used drove.
Each gust that roars across the plain
Grips and rattles us threateningly.

A shrivelled hedge with slanting top
Borders a herd-filled field. An old
Stiff-legged shaggy pony moves towards
The only horse he's seen all Winter.

Our cob roams impatiently over the
Thin inadequate grass, melancholy
Heaps of council-dumped gravel,
Trodden weeds and crushed herbs.

Spent dried stems of shepherds purse
Brush the withered groundsel. A tall
Dry teasle rustles softly. My tame
Rabbit chews angelica and clover.

A knarl of beeches fan the angry wind.
On the switchback highway, the rushing
Cars hurry away into the night.
The cattle wind down into the valley.

Farmer and tractor too, go home, down
Into their warm, lighted, cosy hollow.
We are left alone, a-top the world, cold
As the cold stars. Playtoy of the wind.

Time: October
Place: Wiltshire
Romany terms: The Bow-top or Round-barrel waggon we had at the time, has a canvas roof and bears a slight resemblance to a Prairie-schooner. I refer to it as our canvas cradle.
Notes: A horse can travel only so many miles in a day, a fact overlooked by those keen to move recently encamped travellers. It is often essential to stop overnight, half-way on a long journey, wherever that may happen to be.

Part Two

THE TRAVELLING PEOPLE

SORTIN'

When the trolly returns, willing hands off-load
Sacks, bags, and bundles. Something for nothing.
Eager arms tumble silk, satin and linen, old or new,
Clean or soiled, out upon the ground, a riot of rags.

The fusty, musty smell that clings to old clothes
Goes unnoticed at the prospect of new dresses.
Sisters quarrel over a shawl, one 'chops' two scarves
For it. Individual heaps of claims grow swiftly.

Scavengers for worthwhile food, the dogs turn their
Backs on such human folly, but make good use of soft
Bedding while the bonanza lasts. Like their masters
They take what's given with indifferent gratitude.

Each share is taken away, old clothes brought back
In exchange. Then the serious work of sorting begins.
White woollens, coloured woollens, cottons. Afterwards
Protected from rain. Only dry rags are saleable.

All week the work goes on. The mounds under the sheet
Grow until there is a full waggon-load, worth the
Long journey to the rag-yard. Re-cycling waste, a
Necessary link in the chain of the fashion world.

Time: January
Place: Essex
Romany terms: Chop . . . to exchange; Trolly . . . flat four-wheeled cart; Sheet . . . water-proof canvas.
Notes: Only dry rags are accepted, because it was once the cunning custom to allow the rags to become wet and heavy. Rags are sold by weight.

UP WITH THE LARK

It is a king-cup yellow morning
Sun floods field and sky.
The waggon rests villie-deep among
The dew-wet spring grass.
Yellow shutters gleaming, yellow wheels
Surrounded with yellow dandelions.
Safe within private ground we can
Laugh as police cars pass.
Our first meal bubbles in the small
Hoop-handled pot upon the crane.
A chill wind pushes through the thorn
And bridal-white blossom flowers.
The blue smoke is carried across
Over the gate into the lane

Where rooks defy strangers from
Safe lofty towers.

Three open-lots of drab appearance
A trolly and low tan, all asleep.
Only hungry grais, sunbathing juks,
See or care.
Smooth and verdant the lane begins
Then huge mud-ruts bar further entry.
Here we all wait for 'Vises Fair.
The yog leaps and crackles,
Multi-coloured bantams crow
From wooden shafts. Cage-birds
Burst with song. A hen cradles
Her chicks, Easter chicks, all king-cup yellow.

Time: February
Place: Wiltshire
Romany terms: Villie . . . felloe, the wooden rim of cart or waggon wheel; Grai . . . horse;
Juke . . . jukle, dog; Yog . . . fire.
Notes: 'Vises Fair . . . Devises Fair. Travellers often congregate before a Fair, most often
they are not sure of the exact date, so fill-in a few weeks in the area, moving onto the
ground en masse on the correct day.

WAITING

Twigs will break and snap, the
Dogs rise stiff and cold,
Trot silently, prick-eared
Towards the wood.
No badger, fox or hedgehog
Disturbs the sleepy dusk,
It is the men returning,
Belligerent or convivial.

By the embers, singing kettle,
Ready for the sweet tea.
Itinerants have no 'local',
They take their company.

They will climb unsteadily
The waggon steps, roll
Boots off, into the bed,
Hogging the middle.

The women will squeeze in
Beside. Her lullabye
His snores and the cries
Of fractious chavies.

They have sung and cursed,
Laughed and cried.
Spent the money and lie
Unlovely in the bed.

They are not much. Perhaps
Hardly worth waiting for,
But dogs and women know
It's all they have.

Time: December, *Place*: Suffolk
Romany terms: Chavie . . . child.
Notes: Feats of hard drinking have always been admired and the tradition of celebrating every occasion from the end of the working-week to Easter, Christmas, Weddings, Christenings and Fairs, seems unlikely to be allowed to die by the 20th century traveller!

A FEW DAYS OF PEACE

After the town, the village, the roaring road,
Screaming children, thundering trains,
The quiet green lane, fields, wood and
Water-meadow with tinkling stream.
Open space, tree shade, hedge-shield.
Pristine grass and incredible peace.

An open gate, easy level entrance,
No mud, no wind, no rain.
We the wayfarers, wanderers, nomads, travellers,
Have no reason, no right to expect kindness
Hospitality, space to spend the night,
Sympathy, understanding, a second glance.

And yet we can turn, invited into this haven,
Into a welcoming valley. Old-fashioned,
Kindly farmer, horse-lover,
You cannot know how deep is my gratitude.
To have been without, is to value.
How I shall value and remember this harbour!

Time: April
Place: Monmouthshire
Notes: Before the Caravan Act, more travellers than now had at least one private stopping-place. It is only non-travellers who refer to the place where a trailer-caravan rests as a site. A Romany encampment is called a stopping-place or stop. When one traveller meets another, he enquires 'where are you stopped?'

A REST FROM THE ROAD

We have stopped by the winding lane,
Our shafts rest on the green verge.
Secure for the moment in a gated-road.
Rest awhile wheels with the rolling urge!
On the speed-mad four-lane highways,
one is like a frightened hare,
forward compelled . . . too scared
to turn-off from the headlight's beam.

Amiable cows leave their willow
strewn meadow for the milking shed

loosing a thousand flies which
bide with us for the day.
A large pig, like a fat white peapod,
escapes and wishes we would adopt her.
She is driven grunting, disillusioned
back to the farm, unfed and unloved.

Rivalling the ragged-robin, the bullfinch
sings his small repetitive melody in the
songless air. All about are mauve thistles,
Dock, and stray groups of bastard barley
blowing like bleached hair. Over the bristly
wheat a cool swift breeze blows, shaking
the trailer, bowing the fragile poppies,
pulling the puffed clouds like reluctant balloons.

Time: July.
Place: Suffolk
Notes: Gated roads are usually very narrow and were often on estates or with privately
owned land on either side, so that by closing the gates, cattle could be contained in the
fields without there being hedges to the road-side. It is a pity that many of the gates
have rotted away, and only the posts, often with beautiful hand-made hinges, remain.

31

ONCE A TRAVELLER

With ringing hooves and harness a-jingle, the coloured waggons came.
Lurching down the lane, a trap or trolly between each.
Young colts tied behind, lurchers running under.
The leading trotting-pony lifting its hooves high in race-style.
Red morocco trappings a-blaze with silver horse-shoe buckles.
A noisy-shouting-laughing-throng. Raggle-taggle thoughts and
Draggle-tail clothes. Bright gaudy birds of passage.
The green and blue sails of the prairie ships rock past.
Out from his porch runs an old man, a kennex-romany,
Indifferently the last waggon vanishes round the bend,
Only the distant hooves drum like the old man's heart.

Time: June
Place: Worcestershire
Romany terms: Kennex . . . house-dweller.

AFTER THE RACES

This lorry's worser'n the last!
I'm all jarred up an' down
An' sideways. Draughty ole
Cab. I wishes we were there!

How far now Chasey? The baby
Won't sleep, Chasey-boy can't
Stay still two minutes
Together. Bide quiet!

It'll be nice, make a change,
To atch in a green lane after
The A40 an' Pybush just
Off the roundabouts.

Look at Joe's trailer
Swaying about all over the
Road! Those single-wheel
Transits ain't never no good.

You can talk! This motor's
Seen better times. I'm all
Wore out. Where's the puppy?
I can't see him on the back.

He's led in the box wi' Brin,
Don't fret so Mum. I caught
All the banty chicks, every one,
An' Janet 'membered your

Rush broom what you threw
At that gaujo's ole dog.
I wish that gal hadn't broke
Up my bike. I wants a new'un!

We'm turning down the ole
Road now. Plenty of grass fer
Springfield, put 'im on a
Full chain, mind, Chasey.

Look! There's a trailer roof
Through the trees. It's ole
Black Mary! An' there's dear
Ole Boggy an' little Pemberline.

Pull up on steady now, Chasey.
That's Neta's new West Morning Star,
Stainless steel up to the roof,
Nice blinds. Too flashy fer me!

Goooooooooon Nell. You wouldn't say that
If we 'ad one. Alvis 'as seen us!
Look at that nice wheaten lurcher
Reckon we could mate her wi' Brin?

Sam's got a good sort of
Coloured mare, might have
A chop. An L-number plate T.K.
He's come up this year.

Speak up Nell! Where d'you
Want the trailer? Pull up by
Neta, Chasey. Come on, you
Can have a talk wi' Sam, later.

Roman! Leave the pup, help
Unhitch. Get the spade Chasey-boy,
I want it level. We don't want
To look like Irishmans.

Don't put Springfields too
Close t'Sam's mare. Hello Alvis!
Tell yer Dad I'll be over
When we've had a cup o'tea.

We've come from Epsom. Who
Put the baby's pram in all
That tar? Where's the pin an'
'Ammer to? See you Alvis.

Get the china up Janet, afore
Neta comes. Jest look at her
Worcester vases! Put the new
Satin cushions in the window.

Nice bit o' cosh here, get the
Fire going Chasey-boy, or we'll
Never git no Sunday dinner.
Koshti place this, not too wild.

Time: August
Place: Kent
Romany terms: Chasey-boy . . . son of Chasey; Box . . . dogbox, kennel; Led in . . .
lying down in; Janet . . . pronounced Jaynit; Full-chain . . . whole length of tether;
Boggy . . . nickname for Caradoc; West Morning Star . . . Westmorland Star caravan;
Coloured mare . . . Skewbald; Irishmans . . . Irish Tinkers; Cosh . . . firewood;
Koshti . . . good; Wild . . . lonely or remote.

THE DREAMER

The paper roses are made. Dipped
    In hot wax and tied to fresh
Privet leaves. When the girl returns
    Tomorrow, it will be to another
Place. While she and her blond
    Sister, the white-headed gal
Are out 'calling', the men
    Will move the waggons on.
There will be no secret signs
    Left by the cross-roads—
Stopping-places, now so few,
    Offer little choice!

At none will she be welcome.
    When she carries the basket
Home, now heavy with food,
    Under the loaves will be
Clothes 'for the baby'.
    Perhaps a change of scarf
Or stockings. As these are
    Put upon the hedge,
It will be under the baleful
    Eye of the housewife
Pegging superior washing
    Upon a rotary dryer.

She will mix only with her
    Own, and marry one whom
Nearly all men will hate,
    And dream, but only dream,
Of other ways of life.

Time: March, *Place*: Gloucestershire

HERE TODAY AND GONE TOMORROW

The green lies bruised yet springing
    with tough dandelions.
Wheel-tracks of wide lorries and trailers
    cross to the road.
Up into the young morning air drifts
    stick-fire smoke.
The Travelling People have gone, moved-on,
    only the sparrows
Cease their short song to feast on
    discarded scraps.

Time: October
Place: Hertfordshire
Romany terms: Stick-fire . . . A fire of sticks and branches on the ground. The tell-tale circle of burnt earth, according to its size, denotes whose fire it was. Tramps have relatively small fires, the hedger a huge one, whereas the Gypsy fire is larger than the first (and those one sees in western films) and is either a 'cooking' or women's fire, or a 'social' fire. In either case it is a professional affair, built to stay in, in the rain or wind, and to last.

Part Three

ITINERANTS

THE WAYFARER

Grain green-sequinned, shimmers
In the fresh April wind.
Grey, white, and black clouds
Pull across the forget-me-not sky.

Leafless man-sculptured hedge
Holds tortured twisted arms,
Hand grasping neighbour, to ring
The infant harvest safe.

Mysterious circular dells
Dot viridescent hills, shielding
The brilliant plumage of
Proud young cock pheasants.

Cloud shadows open and close
Riding the prickled gorse.
The lark loses and regains
His empyrean heights.

Onto the narrow road, steps
The wayfarer, moving across
The miles with measured tread,
Eyes narrowed to the sun.

Time: April
Place: Essex
Notes: There is a spiritual comradeship between those who genuinely travel the roads
with 'no fixed abode'. Contrary to common supposition, diverse members of the com-
plicated hierarchy do not mix. At fairs and social gatherings, various classes of traveller
even those of the Romany fraternity, use different public houses, or congregate at different ends of the room, or in different bars.

THE HEDGEMUMPERS

Squat and square the faded green tent, patched
bulging, firmly on the ground.
Drawn up close a hand-painted cut-down lorry,
doors drunkenly swinging, mournful and shabby.
The rough-coated dog, chained and entangled,
whose parents lay between wooden waggon-wheels,
born on the roads, bed unknown, bowl the earth,
walks . . . the long miles tied to the rack.

Seven o'clock, down the winding farm track
echo the rough deep voices of the men,
backs bent, calloused hands clutching new-made
handles, arms hacking, watches ticking, as they hoe.
Crinkled elms and chestnuts throw long black
lazy morning shadows, across the rustic scene
while the men begin another row, and another.

On the waste ground a Dutch Barn dwarfs the tan,
Broken concrete, rotting timber lies everywhere.
A woman emerges, leading a tiny child,
both dressed in clean rags. Her slim figure
wears a black pinna and tartan dress.
The sun catches the gold of their hair.
The rough dog flags his tail, ever hopeful.

Time: July
Place: Cambridgeshire
Romany terms: Tan . . . 'Atching-tan, stopping-place; Hedgemumpers . . . a term for
those who follow a lowly occupation, and used in a derogatory sense for those doing
seasonal farm-work.

OLD MAN AT THE FIRE

Above the cracked lined earth,
His cracked lined face
Rests upon his cracked lined hands.

Around the blackened pot,
His blackened fingers
Fumble above the black tin plate.

His grey hair streams into the
Grey mist-drizzle as upward
Swirl the grey smoke patterns.

No red glow of warm livingroom,
New red scarf and gloves,
One card or red holly berries.

Time: Christmas
Place: Southampton
Notes: The above poem describes how one old man spent Christmas day. When waste
land was opposite the docks, it was home to many individuals. Whilst on this long
established travellers' stop, I became aware that this forest of dereliction was not only
alive with rodents, but human flotsam housed in the dumped cars among the rubbish.
Once such gentlemen of the road could depend on food and shelter at the festive season,
but this Southampton house, like many another, was closed.

THE HIERARCHY

Splendid coach-built travellers' trailers
Stand a-glitter with stainless steel sides,
Cut-glass windows, Nottingham lace curtains.
An island of opulence among less wealthy
Cousins grouped on the ancient common.

New forward-control, custom-cab lorries
With immaculate irridescent paintwork,
Custom-made polished wood bodies,
Double number plates and special pull-bars.

They stand cooling after a day's work.
Twin flex leads from heavy duty batteries
To the television sets. Boys and men sort
The various grades of metals and scrap iron.

When an area has been called by the top
Scavangers, usually long-distance professional
Travellers, successful and self-supporting,
They choose to, and are glad to move-on.

No sooner has their last flashy trailer
Vanished from sight, when men and boys from
Old but good quality trailers, leave their
Rough lorries, and with seeming nonchalance
Walk across, search, find and carry off spoils.
A broken chromium chair, half an alloy ladder.

When they have departed, after an interval,
Boys appear from a ring of local travellers,
All born on or near the Lord's Woods Common.
Travelling only when forced, within the area.

After them, children left at home, appear
And further dismantle an abandoned Ford Cortina,
Roll away old tyres, a pair of platform boots,
A front seat to put down by the outside fire.

When all have left, out from a static
Trailer, lop-sided, green with age,
With smashed windows, comes a boy of
Traveller-stock, his parents failures.

He carries home that which even the rough
Travellers found too far gone, too broken.
His family never move if they can avoid it,
Their names optimistically on a housing-list.

Now the 'rubbish' left by the travellers
Is much reduced. Only the husk of a car
Remains, and scattered, broken junk. Dogs
Come and carry off all things edible.

From some Council houses, an old motorbike
And aged side-car arrives. The shabby driver
Gleans an assorted load he finds worth taking.
Now surely all of any kind of usefulness is gone.

But no, a man in a clean but over-large suit,
Comes on a push-bike, and from a carrier
Takes spanner and hammer. He sets about a
lump of steel, departing an hour later.

In the gathering dusk, a small crooked figure
Limps towards the place, bends painfully among
The debris. His wizened head is encased in
Knitted helmet, moth-holed like his mittens.

Lights appear in the living-trailers and
Near-by houses. Electricity, calor-gas and
Candles. Food and warmth and light, for all
But the lone knarled Searcher, scavenging.

Time: September
Place: Hampshire
Romany terms: Metals . . . non-ferrous metal, such as copper or brass; Flashy . . . Very
expensive trailer; Called . . . worked-over or done; Top . . . Elite or high-ranking.
Notes: People are concerned with ecology. Much is said about the litter that travellers
leave, but little is written about why it is left, and so conspicuously.

Rubbish dumps are an archaeologist's delight, reflecting as they do, the opulence or
otherwise of the age. This affluent society throws away more, more often. Scrap-
collecting travellers could once stop on many more commons, and could therefore move
far more **often; it follows** that there was a smaller amount of leavings, which the gorse
bushes hid while it rotted. Forced to stop on more open roadside ground and to collect
far more scrap in order to live at all in these competitive times, eating pre-packed and
tinned food, there is more waste. Not all travellers leave rubbish, but the invisible is not
seen or photographed.

THE LONG-DISTANCE ROADSTER

There is ME and my tired eyes
And the dazzle of Macadam's brain-child under my thin soles
The meaningless morse of distant wing-mirrors
Moving flecks on grey specks
A long ways away from ME.

Fleshless pylon fingers hold their beadless necklaces
Buzzing like computerised bees
Above my poor head.
And there is ME lying in the grass by the overpass
Stealing the verge from the sparrow-hawk
He hunts and fends fer hisself, like ME.
Now there's a bird to admire.

There is ME and my cramped hands
And that pain what comes and goes in me left leg.
Go away pain, I'll will you off
Same as before.
Down he comes! well that's *his* dinner.

She said to ME, here my man she says,
Here's a bit o'cheese, an' a loaf o'mouldy bread
You can cut off the mould. Spit out
More like, it's everywhere. I wouldn't give it to a dog.
Had a dog once. Company dogs is.
But dogs an' roads don't marry.
Presently I'll try old Will's trick.

Old Will likes Devon, hill an' all,
Now there's a man as never starves. He finds a good pull-in
For motors and lies down by 'is fire,
Head right near the road.
Cars stop alright. I bet he's eatin' bacon right now.

Time: July, *Place*: Hampshire
Notes: Many are the short and long-distance tramps that we know by sight and to speak
to, but not always by name. One observes a certain code of natural manners on the road,
names are not asked.

Mostly 'loners', they are either very talkative, thirsting after human interest and con-
versation, or (as is usually the case with people very taken up with themselves) talking
only of their own doings and never asking questions or showing any interest in others.

THE TRAVELLING BOY

Hot leaf-curling sun
Gold glistening wings of
Vivid butterflies among
The river peppermint.

Across the sky of
Bobbing thistledown,
Young swallows in their
First freedom fly.

The shoals of tiny fish
Have thinned, those left
Are now a finger long,
Wise and self-assured.

The boy sits fishing,
All thoughts but one
Lost amid the reeds;
Like any other boy.

His rod is a hazel wand,
His line, old rick-twine.
His hook, a rusty safety-pin,
But the day . . . the day is HIS.

Time: July
Place: Cornwall
Notes: Travelling boys do not have as great a knowledge of nature as has been wishfully accorded them. They have become more towny than countrified and have no teachers. The romantic build-up around 'the Gypsies' as ace-herbalists, is but a legend lingering as their old-fashioned dress lingered, from the days when most country people had no alternative but to learn and teach their children the free medicines of the hedgerow. Almost all of this knowledge, with a few exceptions of simple canine and equine cures, has been lost. But the country pursuits of hare-coursing, rabbit-shooting and fishing still persist.

Part Four

FLOWER POEMS

WINTER SLEEP (The Mallow)

Pink and imposing were the flowers
Of the Tree Mallow,
Under Summer's benign hand.
The green stems are woody now, tough
And brown where once the flowers
So brightly flounced.

Seedy circled heads lean in
Aged dignity against
Winter's quiet and solemn wood.
Secret life lies in the silent earth
Wasps and wispy butterflies wait
To regain gaudy splendour.

Time: November, *Place*: Sussex

THE WILD ROSE

Exquisite fragility
Born of spiny wood.

Splendid fleeting beauty
Perched on thorny arch.

Golden-hearted ring
Of delicate fragrance.

Summertime gift
Of visual delight.

Each year anew,
Moves me to wonder.

Notes: The wild rose or eglantine, now often falls a victim to the power-driven hedge-cutter, so that the dishes of fragrant flowers tend to blossom close to the foliage of the hedge. Since the closing of many railway lines, many plants can flourish in a natural manner, not the least, the rose, often only seen in its untamed rampant splendour, a truly remarkable and rare sight, in such a setting.

OLD MAN'S BEARD

The fading cloak of traveller's joy
Hangs in hoary mildewed green.
Its undulating furry drapery
Upon a jungle creepered screen.

Time: September, *Place*: Oxfordshire

POPPIES

When the petals of the scarlet poppy
Crimp and fall,
When the bee clings in fluffed stupor
Secret honeyed-world,
A dream of azure flowers and
Sweet swirling nectar scents.

Then the long summer shall pass
Like the haywain,
Along the narrow lane, drifts torn
From the heavy loads
Spangling the high banks
Like bright desperate thought-strands.

When the silver wings of spent plume-moths
Fall to earth and
The topmost bells of the foxglove open,
Then the hen-harrier soars higher
To plummet and strike again
Into another innocent heart.

Then red runs the blood of the victim
Onto the branch and the scarlet flowers.

Time: September, *Place*: Sussex

Part Five

LOVE POEMS, FOR DOMINIC

LOVE INDESTRUCTIBLE

Through the softly draped silk folds of time
winds the golden thread of lasting love.
Holding fast the ties of two alone, who
wandered bright-eyed from the world
journeying across the sylvan wastes.

Companion souls of shadow-wanderings,
Hand of compassion, hand of understanding
giving to each other bounteous life.
Soft glitter-housed the indestructible seeds
awake, awaking beneath the darkened crust.

AWAK'NING

Light as thistle-down your kiss
alights on my heated brow,
yet from sleep I rouse
to see your eyes with tears
of love quick-filling.

Cool as air above the pebbly brook
light the touch of your hand,
calling me from dreams
to beautiful reality,
long dream of vast delight.

SERENITY

Shimmer shimmer the quick-silver
of your love,
take all I have to offer, all
that is me;
I can have no love, nor yet glance
left to spare.

When I ride the wind on your arms
of infinite love,
the journey with our souls, bodies
fast entwined;
I know why we never have the need
to seek assurance.

Like the endless caressing of the
smooth shore
by the rough, yet gentle tide, I have
been born
of your love. What vast store
have you awakened?

DEAREST

The shadows fall, the shadows fall,
bright your sun upon my wall.
My wings are held, I cannot fly,
I give an agonising cry;
Say you heard me, say you heard!
You were my funny nesting-bird,
I fed you once, and you fed me.
Our world it was a storm-tossed tree.
The waving wind takes up my sigh,
for love that lives will never die.
Alone I weep while no bird sings,
glide back to me on silent wings.
Leave the false fruit of delight
life is day as well as night.
One cannot live in dreams alone,
accept the fact you've always known.

ON THE CASTLE WALL

You placed upon my head, the coronet of thorny-flowers.
Garlanded me with festooned, beribboned powers,
sent me forth to run the gauntlets of grief and shame,
gave me your colours, to fight battles in your name.
You sat in audience, around the field of war,
detached from all the rivulets of gore,
in mock defence, lest your bastion fall,
you floated out upon the silver sound of trumpet-call.

I should like to end this book with some verses written for me by Dominic in 1950. We have had our share of joy and sorrow, and been 'delayed by subtle masks', but the early forging of strong mental bonds is always the best foundation for true love.

TO MY L. FROM YOUR L.

I sought for you, long by subtle masks delayed,
Fair shapes I thought were you—
All the world's long roads have not a part with those
You make within the golden day.

The rusted dirk bit home with jagged teeth, and struck
Our mutual wound, and we had wed—
In early primitive splendour beneath the pale-faced,
Lemon-eyed, child moon.

If there were a rainbow, it would frame your golden
Hair against the sky;
I know there will be joy for you and I, of a kind
No sorrow can destroy.

WAGGONS AND TRAILERS

If you are interested in our caravans you may like to know the following. Those wooden and horse-drawn are called *waggons*, those aluminium and motor-drawn, *trailers*, never caravans or vans. Those professionally built share with the early sailing-ship designs incorporating beauty of line, pleasing proportion and artistic decoration combined with practicality. Reading, Ledge, Burton and Bow-top are the main waggon shapes. These became famous through either the original place of building or their coachbuilders. The prototypes were often copied by other waggon-builders, when commissioned to do so, who added their names; for example, the Reading was established by Samuel Dunton of Reading, but among many others, Williams of Bedford and Watson of Derby built Reading waggons. In 1877, the sum of £80 would have purchased a reasonable vardo, to-day, for £3,000 it would not be possible to build an exact copy.

There have always been some Romanies more wealthy than others. In the days when contemporary paintings showed the splendid 'Gypsy Caravan', there were hundreds of families in rough carts, less picturesque and seldom depicted! Unfortunately for the travellers, ignorance of the facts causes wrong conclusions and the erroneous supposition that *only* those with spectacular waggons are the 'real' Gypsies.

Coachbuilders who built for the travellers also took orders for horse-drawn living-waggons for showmen, those connected with circuses and fairs. These vehicles, which only superficially share exterior and interior characteristics with travellers' waggons are quite often sold to the uninitiated as 'genuine gypsy caravans'; their special modifications are apparent to the expert, as indeed are those few surviving specimens which we refer to as mawkens—scarecrows—the mostly unbeautiful, classic follies, built for the gaujes or non-traveller (I have an amusing collection of photographs). Many of these 'gentlemen's caravans' were among the first members of the now famous Caravan Club, established in 1907, and whose badge still bears the horseshoe.

It would be improper not to mention that there were also brush-waggons, an ingenious home-cum-business premises used by the 'broom-squires', the former no longer extant, but well known to the more house-bound wife of pre-1920, from which the door-to-door salesman sold mats, baskets and brooms. There were also more spiritual salesmen, the preachers of small religious sects who toured in their horse-drawn pulpits. Some Jehovah's Witnesses bought one of ours for the same purpose, as late as 1960. A fairly recent waggon which evolved as builders adapted to the travellers' needs for a faster, light-weight, smaller horse or pony waggon, is the much favoured Open-lot. Built like a bow-top but sometimes with a square canvas tilt, with an open front. Canvas curtains close for bad weather. These are by no means plain waggons, having masses of butterfly chamfering, which originated in a practical endeavour to cut away all surplus wood from the edges of battens etc., which luckily has such a decorative effect when emphasised by multi lining-out.

Early motor-drawn trailers followed the shapes of Pullman cars, but inside the traditional waggon lay-out; many were delightful. While showmen harnessed steam to their roundabouts and pulled increasingly larger three-roomed trailers, travellers' maximum size had to be that manageable by the early motor vehicle. It remained, by preference, a trailer of one room until 1969, when a hitherto gaujo-make of trailer broke into the travellers' trailer market with a lightweight model with an end-bedroom. Its entry was fortuitous at a time when the fashion was for regal homes so encrusted with stainless steel and cut-glass (interior wood had given way to heavy formica, even drawers and cupboards were lined) that even the three ton lorries had all they could do to move them in hilly country. Travellers' motor vehicles go through yearly fashions; thus many appendages, such as racks, rails, decorative division of colours, varnished or polished-oak bodies, are 'in' or 'out'. The mere glimpse of a semicircular step-drawbar plus two number plates, immediately marks the Romany lorry. Over the years, these have carried such affectionate nick-names as, Showknees, Mouthorgan, Brazenfaced, Threepennybit, Frogfronted, and Tipcabford. One car-breaker's vehicle earned its owner a life-long nickname derived from the lifting-gear, Hiab John!

The main builders of travellers' trailers specialise in these alone, which are quite unlike any other trailer-caravans, and are made to order. There is often a long waiting list at Mr Vickers of Solihull, John Heath of Penrith, and Sambrooks of Staffordshire. Other firms have what they describe as a 'showman's special' for travellers. A splendid example, nicknamed the zebra trailer, from its numerous stripes of in-lay work, can change hands for fourteen thousand pounds, second-hand. In time such examples will be museum pieces.

Beshlie